Published in 2017 in the U.S. and Canada by
The Word Among Us Press
Frederick, Maryland 21704
www.wau.org

ISBN: 978-1-59325-319-6

Copyright © 2017 Anno Domini Publishing
www.ad-publishing.com
Text copyright © 2017 Angela M. Burrin
Illustrations copyright © 2017 Andrew Everitt-Stuart

Publishing Director: Annette Reynolds
Art Director: Gerald Rogers
Pre-production: Doug Hewitt

Printed and bound in China
May 2017

God
Is Listening
to Me

My Book of
Catholic Prayers

Compiled by Angela M. Burrin

Illustrated by Andrew Everitt-Stewart

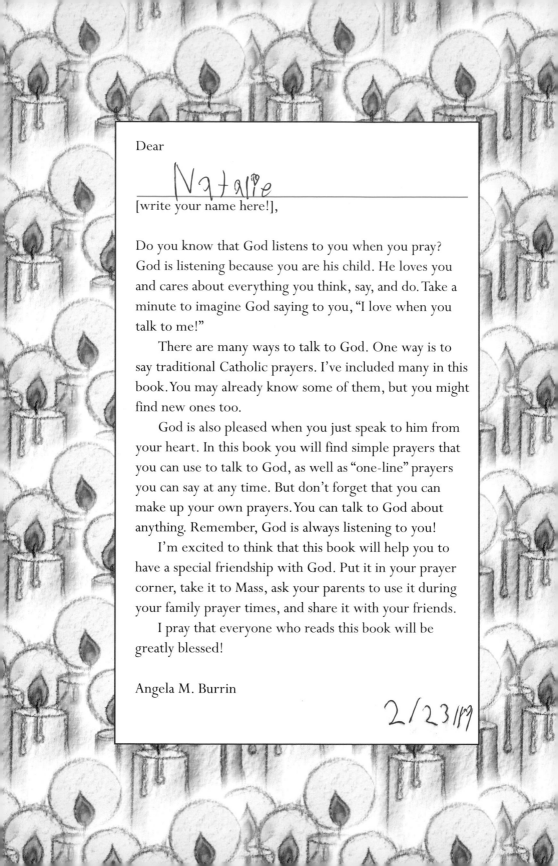

Dear

___Natalie___

[write your name here!],

Do you know that God listens to you when you pray? God is listening because you are his child. He loves you and cares about everything you think, say, and do. Take a minute to imagine God saying to you, "I love when you talk to me!"

There are many ways to talk to God. One way is to say traditional Catholic prayers. I've included many in this book. You may already know some of them, but you might find new ones too.

God is also pleased when you just speak to him from your heart. In this book you will find simple prayers that you can use to talk to God, as well as "one-line" prayers you can say at any time. But don't forget that you can make up your own prayers. You can talk to God about anything. Remember, God is always listening to you!

I'm excited to think that this book will help you to have a special friendship with God. Put it in your prayer corner, take it to Mass, ask your parents to use it during your family prayer times, and share it with your friends.

I pray that everyone who reads this book will be greatly blessed!

Angela M. Burrin

2/23/19

This book belongs to

Natalie
_____

Given on

Grammy
_____

By

2/28/19
_____

Contents

Chapter 1

God, Who Are You?

PRAYING TO THE TRINITY

"God saw everything he had made, and indeed, it was very good."
(Genesis 1:31)

Who is God? God is the Father, the Son, and the Holy Spirit. He is three persons in one God. The Father created the world, and he created you. His Son, Jesus, came to earth. Jesus performed many miracles and taught us about his Father in heaven. He died on the cross for our sins so that we could be forgiven. Then he rose from the dead and is now alive and living in our hearts! The Holy Spirit was sent into the world by Jesus to help us to love God and one another. When you were baptized, you received the Holy Spirit and became part of God's family.

Here are two prayers to the Trinity—
the Father, Son, and Holy Spirit.

The Sign of the Cross

In the name of the Father,
and of the Son,
and of the Holy Spirit.
Amen.

The Glory Be

Glory be to the Father,
and to the Son,
and to the Holy Spirit.
As it was in the beginning,
is now, and ever shall be,
world without end.
Amen.

Here is the prayer that
Jesus taught his disciples.

The Our Father

Our Father, who art in heaven,
hallowed be thy name;
thy kingdom come,
thy will be done
on earth as it is in heaven.
Give us this day our daily bread,
and forgive us our trespasses
as we forgive those who trespass against us;
and lead us not into temptation,
but deliver us from evil.
Amen

A Prayer to the Holy Spirit

Holy Spirit, I'm happy that when I was baptized
I received you into my heart.
You are my special helper.
When I find it difficult to be kind, obedient, or honest,
you give me special graces to make good choices.
Thank you for helping me to love Jesus. Amen.

Come Holy Spirit,

Come, Holy Spirit,
fill the hearts of your faithful,
and kindle in them the fire of your love.
Send forth your Spirit,
and they shall be created.
And you shall renew the face of the earth.
Amen.

The Divine Praises

Blessed be God.
Blessed be his Holy Name.
Blessed be Jesus Christ, true God and true Man.
Blessed be the Name of Jesus.
Blessed be his Most Sacred Heart.
Blessed be his Most Precious Blood.
Blessed be Jesus in the Most Holy Sacrament of the altar.
Blessed be the Holy Spirit, the Paraclete.
Blessed be the great Mother of God, Mary most Holy.
Blessed be her Holy and Immaculate Conception.
Blessed be her glorious Assumption.
Blessed be the name of Mary, Virgin and Mother.
Blessed be Saint Joseph, her most chaste spouse.
Blessed be God in his Angels and in his Saints. Amen.

A Prayer of Thanksgiving for My Baptism

When did you receive the Sacrament of Baptism? If you were a baby when you were baptized, perhaps you have never thanked God for the graces you received. Here's a prayer you can say right now!

I thank you, Jesus, that . . .
Our special friendship began when I was baptized.
My heavenly Father loves me and calls me his beloved child.
The Holy Spirit lives in me and I now have new life.

I praise you, Jesus, that . . .
Original sin was washed away in the waters of Baptism.
I am a member of the Catholic Church.
My parents and godparents are teaching me about the Catholic faith.

I love you, Jesus.
You are my Good Shepherd.
You died on the cross for my sins.
Every day I want to do what
pleases you.

I trust you, Jesus.
I give you my heart.
You are alive and always with me.
You will never stop loving me!
Amen.

Chapter 2

Good Morning, Jesus!

PRAYING WHEN YOU WAKE UP

"Let the little children come to me."
(Mark 10:14)

Praying just means talking to God. You can pray anywhere and at any time. Remember, Jesus loves you and is listening to you. He wants to be your friend. So each morning after you wake up and before you jump out of bed, say, "Jesus, good morning. I love you."

A fun place to pray is in your very own "prayer corner." You could make one in your bedroom. Put a small crucifix there, along with your Bible, your rosary, and some pictures of Jesus. What else could you add?

Five Minutes in My Prayer Corner

Here are some things you can do
when you pray:

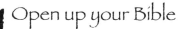

1 Open up your Bible

Read one of your favorite stories. Ask yourself:
What did I like best about the story?
What will I remember about it?

2 Praise and thank God

Father, I praise you for [mention something].
Jesus, I thank you for [mention something].

3 Pray for someone

Jesus, please help _____ today.

4 Listen to the Holy Spirit

Ask the Holy Spirit, "What do you want me
to do for you today?" Then listen!

Here are some other prayers you can pray in the morning.

Psalm 118

This is the day the Lord has made;
    let us rejoice in it and be glad.
You are my God, I give you thanks;
    my God, I offer you praise.
Give thanks to the Lord, for he is good,
    his mercy endures forever.

A Prayer Offering My Day to Jesus

Jesus, thank you for this new day.
I will be doing lots of fun things today.
I want to please you in everything I do.
I don't want to be so busy that I forget you.
I know you won't forget me!
Jesus, whether I'm happy, sad,
excited, angry, worried,
or finding it hard to forgive someone,
I know you will be with me
to guide me and help me. Amen.

A Prayer to My Guardian Angel

Angel of God, my guardian dear,
to whom God's love commits me here,
every day be at my side,
to light and guard,
to rule and guide. Amen.

Chapter 3

Here I Am Again!

PRAYING DURING THE DAY

"You are my help, O Lord!"
(Psalm 70:5)

Have you ever counted up how many people you speak to during the day? You talk to your parents and your brothers and sisters, but also your friends, your teachers at school, and perhaps your grandparents on the phone. Who is missing? God! Throughout your day, you can turn your mind and heart to the Father, to Jesus, and to the Holy Spirit.

A Prayer When I'm Sick

Jesus, I'm not feeling well.
I'll try to do everything I'm told to do
so that I get better quickly, even if I don't like it.
Jesus, I know you healed many people.
Please heal me and all the children
who are sick today. Amen.

A Prayer When I Don't Get My Way

Holy Spirit, I didn't get my way,
and I'm feeling angry inside.
I'm sorry for being selfish right now.
I know I can't always get what I want.
Help me to be thankful for all the good things
you give me every day. Amen.

A Prayer Before a Test

Jesus, I'm about to take a test.
I've studied hard, but I feel a little worried.
One of your miracles was calming the stormy seas.
Calm me right now and give me your peace.
Holy Spirit, during the test,
help me to read carefully,
think clearly, and answer the questions as best I can. Amen.

A Prayer Before I Leave Home

Heavenly Father, I'm just about to leave home.
You know where I'm going
and the people I will meet.
Please be with me in everything I do,
and bring me safely home again. Amen.

A Prayer Before Chores

Holy Spirit, it's that time again—
chore time!
Help me to do my chores as best I can,
without being asked more than once,
and with a smile on my face. Amen.

A Prayer When I'm Afraid

Jesus, I feel afraid of _____
But I know you are more powerful than this fear.
When I say your name, I don't feel so afraid.
Thank you, Jesus, for being with me always. Amen.

A Prayer to Forgive Someone

Jesus, I'm feeling hurt,
and I'm finding it hard to forgive.
You knew what it was like to be hurt,
but you always forgave everyone.
I choose to forgive _____
Help us to be friends once again. Amen.

A Prayer When Visiting a Church

Jesus, I just popped into church to say hello.
I can see the red light in the lamp
next to the tabernacle, so I know you're there.
I'm sure you're happy to see me
because you said, "Let the little children come to me."
So here I am! Please bless me, my family,
and all the people who have no one to pray for them.
Amen.

The Angelus

This is a prayer to say at noon.

The angel of the Lord declared unto Mary:
    And she conceived of the Holy Spirit.
        Hail Mary . . .

Behold the handmaid of the Lord:
    Be it done unto me
        according to your word.
            Hail Mary . . .

And the Word was made flesh:
    And dwelt among us.
        Hail Mary . . .

Pray for us, O holy Mother of God,
    that we may be made worthy
        of the promises of Christ.
            Hail Mary . . .

Grace Before and After Meals

Heavenly Father, great and good,
we thank you for this daily food.
Bless us even as we pray.
Guide and keep us through the day.
Amen.

....

Bless us, O Lord, and these thy gifts
which we are about to receive
from thy bounty,
through Christ our Lord. Amen.

....

We give you thanks,
Almighty God,
For these and all your gifts
which we have received
from your goodness,
through Christ our Lord. Amen.

Chapter 4

Good Night, Jesus!

PRAYING AT THE END OF YOUR DAY

"They were all filled with the Holy Spirit."
(Acts 2:4)

Before getting into bed, go to your prayer corner or kneel at your bedside. This is your special time with Jesus! Talk to him or say one or two of your favorite prayers. Ask the Holy Spirit to help you look over your day. What were the good things that happened, and what were some things that were not pleasing to Jesus? If you have to ask forgiveness of your mom, dad, brother, or sister, do it before you go to sleep.

A Prayer Before Going to Bed

Jesus, I want to thank you for today.
We did a lot together, didn't we?
What I enjoyed most was …
What I found difficult was …
Now it's time for me to go to sleep.
Holy Spirit, please help me to relax
and get to sleep quickly.
Father, while I'm asleep,
give me happy dreams. Amen.

Now I Lay Me Down to Sleep

Thank you, Lord, for another day,
The chance to learn, the chance to play.
Now as I lay me down to sleep,
I pray the Lord my soul to keep.
Please guard me, Jesus, through the night,
And keep me safe till morning's light.

God, I'm Sorry!

(or you can say the Act of Contrition on page 47)

Jesus, before I go to sleep,
I need to tell you something.
Today I said, thought, and did
some things that were wrong.
Jesus, I'm really sorry.
I know you still love me and forgive me.
You died on the cross for all of my sins.
Father, as I sleep, fill me with your love and grace
so that tomorrow, I will be able to do
what is right and pleasing to you. Amen.

A Prayer Before a Crucifix

*If you have a crucifix in your room,
look up at Jesus hanging on the cross
and say this pray to him.*

Look down upon me,
good and gentle Jesus,
as before you I humbly kneel.
With all my heart,
I pray and ask you to put deep within me
faith, hope, love, true sorrow for my sins,
and a desire to please you always.
Amen.

Psalm 23

The Lord is my shepherd;
    there is nothing I shall want.
In green pastures he makes me lie down;
    to still waters he leads me;
    he restores my soul.
He guides me along right paths
    for the sake of his name.
Even though I walk through the valley
    of the shadow of death,
    I will fear no evil, for you are with me;
    your rod and your staff will comfort me.
You set a table before me
    in front of my enemies;
You anoint my head with oil;
    my cup overflows.
Indeed, goodness and mercy will follow me
    all the days of my life;
And I will dwell in the house of the Lord
    all the days of my life.

Chapter 5

My Heavenly Mom

PRAYING TO MARY

"Do whatever he tells you."
John 2:

Mary was specially chosen by God to be the Mother of Jesus. She is your Mother too, and you are her child! Mary is now in heaven with Jesus. There are many prayers to Mary, but you can also talk to her like you would to your mom. She will go to Jesus and tell him what you need.

The Hail Mary

Hail Mary, full of grace, the Lord is with you.
Blessed are you among women,
and blessed is the fruit of your womb, Jesus.
Holy Mary, Mother of God, pray for us sinners,
now and at the hour of our death. Amen.

The Hail, Holy Queen

Hail, holy Queen, Mother of mercy,
our life, our sweetness, and our hope.
To you do we cry, poor banished children of Eve.
To you do we send up our sighs,
mourning, and weeping in this valley of tears.
Turn then, most gracious advocate,
your eyes of mercy toward us, and after this our exile,
show unto us the blessed fruit of your womb, Jesus.
O clement, O loving, O sweet Virgin Mary.
Pray for us, O Holy Mother of God,
that we may be made worthy of the promises of Christ.
Amen.

The Rosary

Praying the Rosary is a beautiful way to think about the birth, life, death, and resurrection of Jesus. Begin by making the Sign of the Cross, and then say the Apostles Creed while holding the crucifix. On the short string, pray an Our Father and three Hail Marys and end with a Glory Be. Then choose to pray one of the four sets of mysteries on the next page. Say the mystery. Pray an Our Father, ten Hail Marys, and a Glory Be. Then go to the next mystery. When you get to the medal on your rosary after the five decades are completed, you can pray the Hail, Holy Queen. All these prayers are in this book. You can also decide to pray just one decade (one Our Father and ten Hail Marys). Mary will be so pleased that you are thinking about her Son!

The Joyful Mysteries— prayed on Mondays and Saturdays

1. The Annunciation (Luke 1:26-38)

   The angel Gabriel tells Mary that she will have a son named Jesus.
2. The Visitation (Luke 1:39-56)

   Mary visits her cousin Elizabeth. Elizabeth's son will be
   John the Baptist.
3. The Birth of Jesus (Luke 2:1-19)

   Jesus is born in a stable in Bethlehem.
   Shepherds and kings visit him.
4. The Presentation (Luke 2:22-40)

   Mary and Joseph take Jesus to the temple to present him to God.
5. The Finding of Jesus in the Temple (Luke 2:41-52)

   After three days, Mary and Joseph find Jesus teaching
   in the Temple.

The Luminous Mysteries—prayed on Thursdays

1. The Baptism of Jesus (Matthew 3:13-17)

   Jesus is baptized by his cousin John in the River Jordan.
2. The Wedding Feast at Cana (John 2:1-11)

   Jesus changes the water into wine. Mary was there!
3. Jesus Proclaims the Kingdom of God (Mark 1:14-20)

   Jesus tells the crowds about God's love and performs miracles.
4. The Transfiguration (Luke 9:28-36)

   Jesus shines like light. God says, "This is my beloved Son."
5. The Institution of the Eucharist (Mark 14:22-25)

   Jesus says, "This is my body" and "This is my blood."

The Sorrowful Mysteries—
prayed on Tuesdays and Fridays

1. The Agony in the Garden (Luke 22:39-46)
   Jesus prays for strength to suffer and die for us.
2. The Scourging at the Pillar (John 19:1-3)
   Jesus is tied to a pillar and cruelly beaten by soldiers.
3. The Crowning with Thorns (Matthew 27:27-31)
   Soldiers put a circle of thorns on Jesus' head.
4. The Carrying of the Cross (Matthew 27:32)
   Jesus falls three times.
5. The Crucifixion (Matthew 27:35-50)
   Jesus dies on the cross..

The Glorious Mysteries—
prayed on Wednesdays
and Sundays

1. The Resurrection (Matthew 28:1-10)
   Jesus rises from the dead.
2. The Ascension (Luke 24:44-53)
   Jesus returns to heaven.
3. The Coming of the Holy Spirit (Acts 2:1-12)
   Jesus sends his Holy Spirit to the disciples.
4. The Assumption of Mary
   Mary is taken up into heaven.
5. The Crowning of Mary (Revelation 12)
   Mary is crowned Queen of Heaven.

A Prayer to Mary, My Mother

When you were a young woman
living in Nazareth,
an angel visited you and asked you
to become the mother of Jesus.
You must have been so surprised.
I'm so glad you said yes!
Now you are my mother too.
So I ask you to watch over me,
and pray for me always.
I know that I can count on you
to bring my prayers to your Son, Jesus.
Thank you for your love and care.
Amen.

Chapter 6

Someone Needs Help, God!

PRAYING FOR OTHERS

"And they came to Jesus, bringing to him a paralyzed man carried by four men." (Mark 2:3)

A great way to help people is to pray for them. You can do this when you are at church, in the car, at home, at school, or with your friends. Remember, you can pray anywhere and at any time! Whenever you see someone who might need help, stop for a moment and say a prayer for that person. Begin to make a list of people to pray for, and put it in your prayer corner.

A Prayer for My Mom and Dad

Jesus, thank you for choosing
my mom and dad to be my parents.
Every day they do so much for me.
When they are tired, worried, or in a hurry,
help them to remember that you are with them.
Keep them safe and well always.
Mary and Saint Joseph, you were Jesus' parents.
Pray for my mom and dad. Amen.

A Prayer for My Brothers and Sisters

Father, thank you for my brothers and sisters
and all the fun we have together.
You know we don't always get along,
so help us to be patient and kind with one another.
We want to be best friends forever! Amen.

A Prayer for People Who Are Sick

Jesus, you love to heal people.
Here's my list of those who are sick:

_____

_____

_____

_____

Just as you healed the paralyzed man
who was lowered down from the roof,
heal these men, women, and children.
Bring them comfort and peace,
and bless all who care for them. Amen.

A Prayer for the Homeless

Jesus, there are thousands of men, women, boys, and girls
all over the world who don't have a home.
Because of wars, some live in refugee camps.
Because of floods and fires, some live in shelters.
Because some can't pay their rent, they live on the streets.
Jesus, please provide for all of their needs. Amen.

A Prayer for Our Pope

Father, thank you for our Pope.
He is very busy,
so please give him lots of energy!
Protect him in all that he does.
Holy Spirit, fill him with wisdom and love
as he guides and leads our Church. Amen.

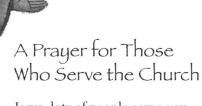

A Prayer for Those Who Serve the Church

Jesus, lots of people serve you—
priests, deacons, sisters
and brothers,
our religion teachers,
and so many more!
I want to thank you especially for

_____

_____

_____

_____

Bless them for all they do. Amen.

Chapter 7

Friends in High Places

PRAYING TO THE SAINTS

"The elders held a harp and gold bowls filled with incense, which are the prayers of the saints." (Revelation 5:8)

The saints loved God. Every saint has a different story to tell. Some died bravely for their faith. Others worked very hard to help the poor. From all over the world, men, women, and even children have become saints. They show us how to grow closer to Jesus. You can ask the saints to pray for you. They are all part of the same family as you—the family of God!

A Prayer to Saint Joseph

Saint Joseph, God gave you a special task—
to care for Mary and Jesus.
You worked as a carpenter to provide for them,
and you protected them from all danger.
Please pray for and watch over my family too. Amen.

The Prayer of Saint Francis of Assisi

Lord, make me an instrument of your peace.
Where there is hatred, let me sow love;
where there is injury, pardon;
where there is doubt, faith;
where there is despair, hope;
where there is darkness, light;
where there is sadness, joy;
O Divine Master, grant that I may not so much
seek to be consoled as to console;
to be understood as to understand;
to be loved as to love.
For it is in giving that we receive;
it is in pardoning that we are pardoned;
and it is in dying that we are born to eternal life.
Amen.

The Breastplate of Saint Patrick

Christ with me,
Christ before me,
Christ behind me,
Christ in me,
Christ beneath me,
Christ above me,
Christ on my right,
Christ on my left,
Christ when I lie down,
Christ when I sit down,
Christ when I arise,
Christ in the heart of every man who thinks of me,
Christ in the mouth of everyone who speaks of me,
Christ in every eye that sees me,
Christ in every ear that hears me. Amen.

A Prayer to Saint Teresa of Calcutta

Saint Teresa of Calcutta, you heard Jesus ask you
to love the poorest of the poor.
When you saw those who were sick
or dying on the streets,
you saw Jesus and cared for them.
Sometimes I'm too busy to see what others need.
But I don't want to think only about myself.
Please pray that I will look out for others
and help them when I can. Amen.

A Litany of the Saints

Mary, Mother of God, pray for us.
Saint Joseph, pray for us.
Saint John the Baptist, pray for us.
Saint Peter, pray for us.
Saint Paul, pray for us.
Saint Stephen, pray for us.
Saint John Bosco, pray for us.
Saint Maximilian Kolbe, pray for us.
Saint Therese of Lisieux, pray for us.
Saint Bernadette, pray for us.
Saint Maria Goretti, pray for us.
Saint Elizabeth Ann Seton, pray for us.
Saint Pope John XXIII, pray for us.
Saint Pope John Paul II, pray for us.
(Add a favorite saint.)
Amen.

A Prayer to My Patron Saint

*Your patron saint is the saint you were named after
or a saint who has a special place in your life.*

Hello, Saint _____
You are my patron saint.
Your life pleased God very much.
I'd like to be a saint too.
Please pray that I follow your example
and love God as you did.
Pray, too, for my family and friends
and for anyone who doesn't
know and love Jesus. Amen..

Chapter 8

Time for Church

PRAYING AT MASS

"Do this in memory of me." (Luke 22:19)

The Mass is a time when Catholics come together to pray, sing, thank God—and receive Jesus in the Eucharist! Here are the prayers of the Mass. Remember, Jesus is listening and is so happy when you are in church with your family.

A Prayer on the Way to Mass

Jesus, sometimes I'm excited to go to Mass,
and sometimes I'm not.
When I'd rather be doing something else,
help me not to be grumpy.
Please don't let me forget that it is you
who will be at church to greet me. Amen.

The Confiteor

I confess to almighty God
and to you, my brothers and sisters,
that I have greatly sinned,
in my thoughts and in my words,
in what I have done and in what I have failed to do,

through my fault, through my fault,
through my most grievous fault;

therefore I ask blessed Mary ever-Virgin,
all the Angels and Saints,
and you, my brothers and sisters,
to pray for me to the Lord our God..

The Gloria

Glory to God in the highest,
and on earth peace to people of good will.

We praise you,
we bless you,
we adore you,
we glorify you,
we give you thanks for your great glory,
Lord God, heavenly King,
O God, almighty Father.

Lord Jesus Christ, Only Begotten Son,
Lord God, Lamb of God, Son of the Father,
you take away the sins of the world,
    have mercy on us;
you take away the sins of the world,
    receive our prayer;
you are seated at the right hand of the Father,
    have mercy on us.

For you alone are the Holy One,
you alone are the Lord,
you alone are the Most High,
Jesus Christ,
with the Holy Spirit,
in the glory of God the Father.
Amen..

The Nicene Creed

I believe in one God,
the Father almighty,
maker of heaven and earth,
of all things visible and invisible.

I believe in one Lord Jesus Christ,
the Only Begotten Son of God,
born of the Father before all ages.
God from God, Light from Light,
true God from true God,
begotten, not made, consubstantial with the Father;
through him all things were made.
For us men and for our salvation
he came down from heaven,
and by the Holy Spirit was incarnate of the Virgin Mary,
and became man.

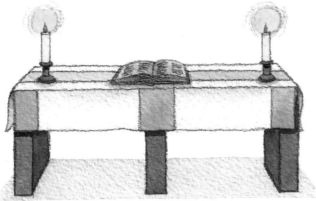

For our sake he was crucified under Pontius Pilate,
he suffered death and was buried,
and rose again on the third day
in accordance with the Scriptures.
He ascended into heaven
and is seated at the right hand of the Father.
He will come again in glory
to judge the living and the dead
and his kingdom will have no end.

I believe in the Holy Spirit, the Lord, the giver of life,
who proceeds from the Father and the Son,
who with the Father and the Son is adored and glorified,
who has spoken through the prophets.

I believe in one, holy, catholic and apostolic Church.
I confess one Baptism for the forgiveness of sins
and I look forward to the resurrection of the dead
and the life of the world to come. Amen.

The Sanctus

Holy, Holy, Holy Lord God of hosts.
Heaven and earth are full of your glory.
Hosanna in the highest.
Blessed is he who comes in the name of the Lord.
Hosanna in the highest.

The Memorial Acclamation

We proclaim your Death, O Lord,
and profess your Resurrection
until you come again.

The Lamb of God

Lamb of God, you take away the sins of the world,
have mercy on us.
Lamb of God, you take away the sins of the world,
have mercy on us.
Lamb of God, you take away the sins of the world,
grant us peace.

Lord, I Am Not Worthy

Lord, I am not worthy
that you should enter under my roof,
but only say the word
and my soul shall be healed.

A Prayer After Communion

Jesus, you are really present in the Eucharist.
Thank you for coming into my heart.
You are holy, awesome, powerful, and kind.
Thank you for my life, my family, my friends,
and the priest who said Mass.
Jesus, what do you want to say to me?
[Take some time to listen!] Amen.

Chapter 9

I'm Sorry, Jesus

PRAYING BEFORE AND AFTER CONFESSION

"Christ died for our sins."
(1 Corinthians 15:3)

When you go to Confession, you meet Jesus there. You won't see him, but you will see the priest. In Confession, the priest takes Jesus' place. The priest received this special privilege when he was ordained.

Sometimes we are ashamed of our sins, but after we confess them, the priest says, "I absolve you from your sins in the name of the Father, and of the Son, and of the Holy Spirit." Remember, Jesus died on the cross for all of our sins. After your Confession, your heavenly Father won't remember them anymore. That should make you very happy!

A Prayer Before Confession

Holy Spirit, I'm about to go to Confession
so I need your help to examine my conscience.
I want to be honest and tell the priest
what I've done wrong.
Thank you, Father, that in Confession,
all my sins will be forgiven and forgotten! Amen.

The Act of Contrition

My God,
I am sorry for my sins with all my hearts.
In choosing to do wrong and failing to do good,
I have sinned against you whom I should love above all things.
I firmly intend, with your help, to do penance, to sin no more,
and to avoid whatever leads me to sin. Amen.

An Examination of Conscience for Children

You can use these questions to help you decide
what sins to confess to the priest.

Have I prayed every day?
Have I prayed my morning prayers and night prayers?
Have I prayed with my parents and family?
Have I been moody and rebellious about praying
    and going to church on Sunday?
Have I asked the Holy Spirit to help me whenever
    I have been tempted to sin?
Have I asked the Holy Spirit to help me do what is right?
Have I been obedient and respectful to my parents?
Have I lied or been deceitful to them or to others?
Have I been arrogant, stubborn, or rebellious?
Have I talked back to parents, teachers, or other adults?
Have I pouted and been moody?
Have I been selfish toward my parents, brothers, and sisters,
    teachers, or my friends and schoolmates?
Have I gotten angry at them? Have I hit anyone?
Have I held grudges or not forgiven others?
Have I treated other children with respect,
    or have I made fun of them and called them names?
Have I used bad language?
Have I stolen anything? Have I returned it?
Have I performed my responsibilities,
    such as homework and household chores?
Have I been helpful and affectionate toward my family?
Have I been kind and generous with my friends?

Psalm 51

This is a psalm that King David wrote to tell God that he was sorry.

God, be merciful to me
    because you are loving.
Because you are always ready to be merciful,
    wipe out all my wrongs.
Wash away all my guilt
    and make me clean again.
I know about my wrongs.
I can't forget my sin.
You are the one I have sinned against.
I have done what you say is wrong.
You want me to be completely truthful.
So teach me wisdom.
Take away my sin, and I will be clean.
Wash me, and I will be whiter than snow.
Make me hear sounds of joy and gladness.
Create in me a pure heart, God.
Make my spirit right again.
Do not send me away from you.
Do not take your Holy Spirit away from me.
Give me back the joy
    that comes when you save me.
Keep me strong by giving me a willing spirit.
Then I will teach your ways
    to those who do wrong.
And sinners will turn back to you.
God, you are the one who saves me.
I will sing about your goodness.

The Chaplet
of Divine Mercy

Eternal Father,
for the sake of His
sorrowful passion,
have mercy on us
and on the whole world.

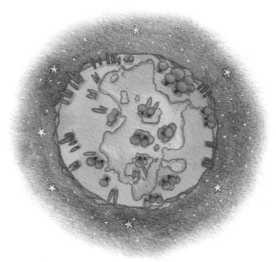

The Jesus Prayer

Lord Jesus Christ,
Son of God,
have mercy on me,
a sinner.

Chapter 10

A Heavenly Home

PRAYING WHEN SOMEONE DIES

"Today you will be with me in Paradise."
(Luke 23:43)

It is always very sad when someone dies. We cry, and our hearts seems to hurt inside of us. We miss that person so much. At the funeral, people talk about that person's life and look at their photos. That reminds us of all the happy times we had together.

Before Jesus ascended into heaven, he said to his disciples, "I am going to prepare a place for you" (John 14:3). Isn't that good news? Jesus, Mary, Joseph, and the saints were born into this world, lived and died, and are now in heaven. You, too, are on a journey to heaven!!

Saints of God

Saints of God, come to his [or her] aid!
Come to meet him, angels of the Lord!
Receive his soul and present him to God the Most High.
May Christ, who called you, take you to himself;
May angels lead you to Abraham's side.

The Eternal Rest Prayer

Give her [or him] eternal rest, O Lord,
and may your perpetual light shine upon her.
May she rest in peace.
May her soul and the souls of all the faithful departed
through the mercy of God
rest in peace. Amen.

A Prayer for Someone
Who Was Close to Me

Jesus, I want to pray for

_____

who has died.
You know how much I loved him [or her].
I miss him very much.
I like to remember the things we did together.
[Take time to do this].
Thank you for all these wonderful memories.
I pray that he will be with you forever in heaven
and that I will see him again one day. Amen..

Chapter 11

Special Prayers for Special Times

PRAYING FOR IMPORTANT DAYS AND EVENTS

"Pray at all times."
(Ephesians 6:18)

Saint Paul was an apostle who told people to pray at all times. Isn't that good advice? Can you think of some special occasions when you can say a prayer? The Father, Jesus, and the Holy Spirit smile when they see you and your family praying, and in return, they pour out more and more love into your hearts.

A Birthday Prayer

Jesus, I'm so excited that it's my birthday. I just want to tell you that I'm _____ years old today! But you know that, don't you?

Jesus, on my birthday, let me say thank you for . . .

        my life,
        my mom and dad,
        everyone in my family,
        my friends,
        and especially you!

Jesus, I know you will be with me every day this year.
Keep me healthy, help me with my schoolwork, and
help me to be obedient and kind.

Jesus, I love you. Thank you for being my friend! Amen..

A Prayer on My First Holy Communion

Jesus, today is our big day!
I'm going to receive you in Communion for the first time.
I'm so excited that you are coming to me.
I can't wait to have you in my heart and talk to you.
I'll tell you that I love you,
and I'll listen to what you have to say to me. Amen.

A Prayer for the Beginning of a New School Year

Jesus, it's back-to-school time.
I'm excited and a little nervous.
There will be lots of new
things for me to learn
and lots of new friends to make.
Bless my teacher and everyone at my school.
Please help me to concentrate during my classes
and do a good job on my homework. Amen.

A Prayer Before a Sports Event

Jesus, there's a big game coming up.
You know that I want to play my best and win.
Please help me to focus on the game and to play fairly.
Don't let anyone get injured. Bless the coaches
and all those who come to watch the game. Amen.

A Prayer Before a Big Trip or Vacation

Father,
I've been counting down the days
until our trip,
and today's the day!
Bless all the preparations that
Mom and Dad are making.
They've got lots to do,
so help them to be peaceful
and not forget anything important.
Please give us a safe trip
and fun times together.
Amen.

Chapter 12

Short and Sweet

ONE-LINE PRAYERS

"Give thanks to the Lord, for he is good."
(Psalm 136:1)

Prayers don't have to be long—they can just be one-line prayers that you say from your heart. Here are some one-line prayers that you and your family can memorize. Then you will always have one in your mind whenever you need it. Or you can write your own one-line prayers and put them in your prayer corner.

Jesus, I love you.

Jesus, I trust in you.

Father, I offer you this day.

Holy Spirit, help me.

Jesus, I'm sorry.

Mary, Mother of God, pray for me.

Father, I praise you.

Jesus, bless my family.

Jesus, stay close to me.

Holy Spirit, show me what to do.

Father, keep me safe.

Jesus, thank you for today..

Dear Parents,

I thought that the last prayer in this book should be one for parents. I think I hear you saying, "Yes, I need prayer!" From my years as a teacher and principal and as the godmother of eleven, I know something of the joys and sorrows, successes and challenges of parenting children and instructing them in the Catholic faith.

So to you—a parent—I urge you to always remember that God loves you. He delights in you. God knows your heart's desire for each of your children. He is always with you, and he loves your sons and daughters more than you do.

Now that this prayer book is in your family, I encourage you to seek the wisdom of the Holy Spirit as to how, where, and when to use it. What works one week may not work for another. Experiment! Be creative and flexible! Enjoy it! And ask your children for ideas on how to use it.

Angela M. Burrin

And now here is a final prayer you can pray:

Father, I need joy, peace, patience, and a deep assuredness of your great love for me and my family. Give me wisdom as I raise my children in the Catholic faith. Help me to find time in my day to listen to your still, small voice. And please let me know that you are always listening to me. Amen.